Cathy & Justin!

Happy Christmas!

May this book "up the ante",
"better the score" & bring
some fun, joyful, loving
"answers."

much love
& care,

Liz

LOVE'S

book of answers

LOVE'S
book of answers

CAROL
BOLT

stewart, tabori & chang ■ new york

Text copyright © 2002 Carol Bolt

Graphic production by KIM TYNER
Cover and book design by NINA BARNETT

Published in 2002 by
Stewart, Tabori & Chang
A company of La Martinière Groupe
115 West 18th Street
New York, NY 10011

Export sales to all countries except
Canada, France, and French-speaking
Switzerland:
Thames & Hudson, Ltd.
181A High Holborn
London WC1V 7QX
England

Canadian Distribution:
Canadian Manda Group
One Atlantic Avenue, Suite 105
Toronto, Ontario M6K 3E7
Canada

Library of Congress
Cataloging-in-Publication Data

Bolt, Carol, 1963-
  Love's book of answers / Carol Bolt.
        p. cm.
    ISBN 1-58479-25-6
Fortune-telling by books. 2. Love—
Miscellanea. I. Title

BF1891.B66 B647 2002
133.3—dc21
2002066826

The text of this book was composed
in Trebuchet
Printed in China
10 9 8 7 6 5 4 3 2 1
First printing

HOW TO USE
LOVE'S BOOK OF ANSWERS

- Hold the book closed and concentrate on your question for
  ten or fifteen seconds. Questions should be closed-ended, e.g.,
  "Should I date my dentist's cousin's brother?" or "Should I ask
  for a commitment?"

- While visualizing or speaking the question, place one hand palm
  down on the book's front cover and stroke the edge of the pages,
  back to front.

- When you sense that the time is right, open the book . . .
  and there will be your answer.

- Repeat the process for as many questions as you have.

let yourself fall hard

cut your losses

allow room for surprises

passionate involvement
will be expected

have another plan
to fall back on

what would it do for you?

emphasize participation

don't push too hard

put all your cards
on the table

there's no time for talking

you'll be miserable
if you settle

it's worth the price

this is no time to be serious

you've got all
the right moves

not so fast; make it last

there is no right or wrong

a headache could be
advantageous

show some nerve

watch out for clinging vines

keep your options open

is this something you'd want
again . . . and again?

play it close to the heart

the outcome could be golden

call now

don't censor yourself

expect something big

it's for real

don't sit on the fence

don't even think about it

kiss now, talk later

make sure you're
the only one

don't wear out your welcome

too much caution won't lead
to happiness

be direct

keep it to yourself

be a better friend

don't forget the competition

start at the bottom and
work your way up

you'll have to compromise

ask for more

don't take the call

you'll want it hot

talk now, kiss later

keep your feet on
the ground

don't be coy

it's time to send flowers

act as if your heart is in it

no

yes

don't get mixed up in it

it could get messy

become your own fantasy

make a game of it

don't be too sentimental

it's bound to last

wait a week

you aren't the only one
who's nervous

you're in hot water;
make bubbles

romance your way into it

make a commitment

expand your view
of pleasure

get fresh

the more the merrier

could prove to be
irresistible

consider it foreplay

be clear about
what you want

get a witness

be persistent

indulge your appetites

start something new

push harder

hold on

charm your way out of it

don't keep any secrets

a third party may not agree

you're going to need a map

don't bite off more
than you can chew

for now, keep it to yourself

wait until you've been asked

set ground rules

use your imagination

be brazen; it's up to you

do what you're told

flirt, flirt, flirt

make it quick

ride it out

don't wait too long

it's not your style

work up a sweat

it's just a phase

try it on top

there are others to consider

giddyup!

modest moves last longer

don't pack your bags

reinvent the fantasy

you're not the only one

it's gonna be sweet

put both of your oars
in the water

it will be harder than
you think

the differences
could be thrilling

take your time;
you'll want this to last

work it out on your own

negotiate a fresh start

there's nothing casual
about it

know when it's time to go

keep your heart in check

there is no logical
explanation

talk about it with
your closest friend

sleep on it

set a date

don't wait to be seduced

you've already
crossed the line

pack your bags

give it up

now or never

it's not what you think

this once, give in

you'll need more space

maybe tomorrow

what are you waiting for?

full steam ahead

the only way to be sure
is to get closer

clear your calendar

wait for the dust to settle

could be good under
different circumstances

you could be in over your head, but what better way to find out?

rub two things together
and see if you can
start a fire

score!

start building a nest

once you're committed,
don't hesitate

you've been in this too long

take a cold shower,
then reconsider

is this what you'd want
for your best friend?

find out more about it

write a blank check

love the one you're with

it could leave you bored

allow the anticipation
to simmer

try everything, but
nothing to excess

wait for a better offer

don't be afraid
to want it all

let yourself fall hard

cut your losses

allow room for surprises

passionate involvement
will be expected

have another plan
to fall back on

what would it do for you?

emphasize participation

don't push too hard

put all your cards
on the table

there's no time for talking

you'll be miserable
if you settle

it's worth the price

this is no time to be serious

you've got all
the right moves

not so fast; make it last

there is no right or wrong

a headache could be
advantageous

show some nerve

watch out for clinging vines

keep your options open

is this something you'd want
again . . . and again?

play it close to the heart

the outcome could be golden

call now

don't censor yourself

expect something big

it's for real

don't sit on the fence

don't even think about it

kiss now, talk later

make sure you're
the only one

don't wear out your welcome

too much caution won't lead
to happiness

be direct

keep it to yourself

be a better friend

don't forget the competition

start at the bottom and
work your way up

you'll have to compromise

ask for more

don't take the call

you'll want it hot

talk now, kiss later

keep your feet on
the ground

don't be coy

it's time to send flowers

act as if your heart is in it

no

yes

don't get mixed up in it

it could get messy

become your own fantasy

make a game of it

don't be too sentimental

it's bound to last

wait a week

you aren't the only one
who's nervous

you're in hot water;
make bubbles

romance your way into it

make a commitment

expand your view
of pleasure

get fresh

the more the merrier

could prove to be
irresistible

consider it foreplay

be clear about
what you want

get a witness

be persistent

indulge your appetites

start something new

push harder

hold on

charm your way out of it

don't keep any secrets

a third party may not agree

you're going to need a map

don't bite off more
than you can chew

for now, keep it to yourself

wait until you've been asked

set ground rules

use your imagination

be brazen; it's up to you

do what you're told

flirt, flirt, flirt

make it quick

ride it out

don't wait too long

it's not your style

work up a sweat

it's just a phase

try it on top

there are others to consider

giddyup!

modest moves last longer

don't pack your bags

reinvent the fantasy

you're not the only one

it's going to be sweet

put both of your oars
in the water

it will be harder than
you think

the differences
could be thrilling

take your time;
you'll want this to last

work it out on your own

negotiate a fresh start

there's nothing casual
about it

know when it's time to go

keep your heart in check

there is no logical
explanation

talk about it with
your closest friend

sleep on it

set a date

don't wait to be seduced

you've already
crossed the line

pack your bags

give it up

now or never

it's not what you think

this once, give in

you'll need more space

maybe tomorrow

what are you waiting for?

full steam ahead

the only way to be sure
is to get closer

clear your calendar

wait for the dust to settle

could be good under
different circumstances

you could be in over your
head, but what better way
to find out?

rub two things together
and see if you can
start a fire

score!

start building a nest

once you're committed,
don't hesitate

you've been in this too long

take a cold shower,
then reconsider

is this what you'd want
for your best friend?

find out more about it

write a blank check

love the one you're with

it could leave you bored

allow the anticipation
to simmer

try everything, but
nothing to excess

wait for a better offer

don't be afraid
to want it all

ACKNOWLEDGMENTS

This book is dedicated to Kris; you are the answer to all of my "love" questions. Thank you.

I want to express my tremendous gratitude to my agents, Victoria Sanders and Chandler Crawford. Thank you for your all your continued hard work— the gift that keeps giving.

Many thank-yous and much gratitude to my slightly outrageous editor, Constance Herndon. Your vision kept me going to better and then to best.

And thanks and much respect to the designer of *Love's Book of Answers*, Nina Barnett, and to its production director, Kim Tyner. You made a hot little book really sizzle! Thank you!

ABOUT THE AUTHOR

CAROL BOLT is a multidisciplinary artist who is also the author of four published books. Bolt's artwork has been widely exhibited around the country and can be found in both public and private collections. She holds a bachelor of fine arts from the University of Delaware and a master of fine arts from the University of Washington. Bolt produced the original *Book of Answers* as an artist's edition of 130 in 1998, and the book was then published commercially later that year; it went on to become a best-seller. She now lives in Seattle.

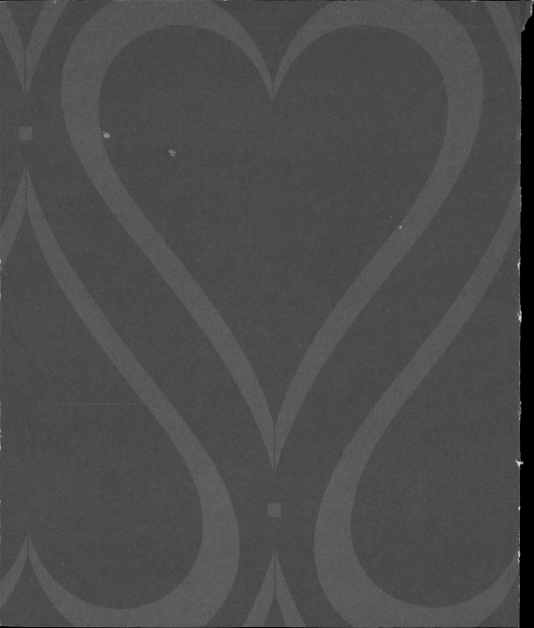